The Story of
ENVIRONMENTALIST
WANGARI MAATHAI

To Cecelia, my grandmother, and all my students, may you take root and flourish—J.C.J.

To my mother, Inez Sadler, and my family, who have supported me unconditionally in my efforts, since childhood, as an artist—S.L.S.

The Story of
ENVIRONMENTALIST
WANGARI MAATHAI

by **Jen Cullerton Johnson**

with illustrations by **Sonia Lynn Sadler**

Lee & Low Books Inc.
New York

Photo credits:
p.11 WildMedia / Shutterstock
p.13 Designua / Shutterstock.com
p.21 Roy Johnson / Alamy Stock Photo
p.33 Pete Oxford / Alamy Stock Photo
p.36 Khalil Senosi / AP / Shutterstock
p.44 Abhi Alwar / Lee & Low Books Inc.
p.49 dpa picture alliance archive / Alamy Stock Photo

LEE & LOW BOOKS Inc., 95 Madison Avenue, New York, NY 10016
leeandlow.com
Edited by Jennifer Fox and Kandace Coston
Book design by Abhi Alwar
Book production by The Kids at Our House
Manufactured in the United States of America by Lake Book Manufacturing, Inc.
The text is set in Vollkorn
The display font is set in Avenir
The illustrations are rendered in scratchboard and oil
10 9 8 7 6 5 4 3 2 1
First Edition
Cataloging-in-Publication Data on file with the Library of Congress
ISBN 978-1-64379-012-1

TABLE OF CONTENTS

CHAPTER ONE

A PROMISE TO PROTECT

"**C**ome," Wangari's mother called. She **beckoned** her young daughter over to a tall tree with a wide, smooth trunk and a crown of green, oval leaves.

"Feel," her mother whispered.

Wangari spread her small hands over the tree's trunk. She smoothed her fingers over the rough bark.

"This is the *mugumo*," her mother said. "It is home to many. It feeds many too."

She snapped off a wild fig from a low branch

and gave it to her daughter. Wangari ate the delicious fruit, just as geckos and elephants did. High in the tree, birds chirped in their nests. The branches bounced with jumping monkeys.

"Our people, the Kikuyu of Kenya, believe that our ancestors rest in the tree's shade," her mother explained.

Wangari wrapped her arms around the trunk as if hugging her great-grandmother's spirit. She promised never to cut down the tree.

Trees and the Forest Ecosystem

A *forest ecosystem* is a natural community of animals and plants that **coexist** together in a woodland environment. All living things within the ecosystem are **interdependent**, meaning they work together and rely on one another to survive. If something goes wrong with one area of the ecosystem, all other areas are affected. Trees are an essential part of a forest ecosystem and play many roles in keeping the environment balanced.

Trees control the climate of a forest. Their large green leaves block the sun's heat and keep the forest and the animals that live within it cool. Leaves also provide shelter for animals, protecting them from rain, harmful **ultraviolet** (UV) **light**, and heavy winds. With enough trees, a forest can even affect wind speed and wind direction!

Trees support **biodiversity** by providing food to many animals. For example, the leaves and branches of African trees give **nourishment** to elephants, monkeys, and giraffes. Birds, bees, bats, and many insects drink the nectar from flowering trees. Animals also eat from fruit trees. Fruits such as apples, figs, and almonds have seeds in them. After the animals digest the fruit, the seeds pass into their waste and fall to the ground, allowing the life cycle of the fruit tree to begin again. Without trees to provide food, all the creatures that depend on the tree would not survive.

A family of owls huddle in the shade of a tree. They rely on the tree for shelter.

Trees also support the plants around them by absorbing **nutrients** and water in the ground. When it rains, tree roots capture and store rainwater underground for later use. Underground water hydrates the tree and helps plants growing near the tree by keeping the soil moist. Tree roots also hold the *topsoil*, the layer of soil closest to the surface, in place. Topsoil is made up of **organic** materials, minerals, water, and air. Healthy topsoil provides nutrients to plants and trees. When trees are cut down, wind and rain can strip away the topsoil. This process is called **erosion** and can cause flooding and mudslides, which negatively affect nearby streams and rivers.

Environmentalists want to protect the forest ecosystem because trees help fight climate change and are key to lessening the *greenhouse effect*. The greenhouse effect occurs when gases in the earth's atmosphere—especially **carbon dioxide** (CO_2)—trap the sun's heat, causing the temperature of the earth's surface and lower atmosphere to rise. When the earth's temperature warms, oceans and seas rise in temperature, too. Warmer oceans and seas melt glaciers, melted glaciers increase sea levels, and increased sea levels can cause **aquatic** creatures to die and **drastically** change weather conditions. Trees help clean the air by absorbing carbon dioxide and other gases from the atmosphere, then releasing oxygen back into the environment for animals and people to breathe. Planting more trees can help improve air quality as well as decrease air pollution and the number of people suffering from **asthma** and other breathing-related illnesses.

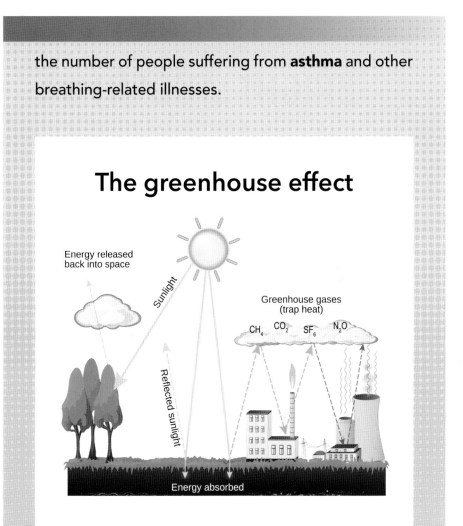

This image shows how the greenhouse effect cycle warms the earth. When sunlight enters Earth's atmosphere, it is absorbed or reflected by the earth. Some of the reflected sunlight is released into space and some of it is trapped by greenhouse gases. Greenhouse gases (such as CH_4, CO_2, SF_8, and N_2O) are generated by power plants and trap the sunlight close to the earth's surface warming the earth and its lower atmosphere.

CHAPTER TWO
BRIGHT STUDENT

Each year the mugumo grew, and so did Wangari. As the oldest girl in her family, she had many chores. Every day she fetched water, clear and sweet, from the river. In the rainy season she planted sweet potatoes, **millet**, and beans. When the sun shone brightly in the dry season, she shooed the chickens into the shade.

Sometimes when her brother, Nderitu, returned from school, he and Wangari played among the arrowroot plants by the stream, where thousands of eggs hatched into tadpoles and tadpoles turned into frogs.

During those times, Nderitu told Wangari what he had learned in his classes. "Plants give air for people to breathe," he said. "Twenty divided by two is ten. There are seven great seas to sail."

Wangari listened as still as a tree, but her mind swirled with curiosity like the currents in the stream. Even though she knew few Kikuyu girls who could read, Wangari dreamed of going to school and learning, just like her brother.

"I must go to school," she told him.

"You will," he promised.

Nderitu talked to their parents. "Why doesn't Wangari go to school?" he asked.

Wangari's parents knew she was smart and a hard worker. Although it was unusual for a girl to be educated, they decided to send her to school. They knew she would not disappoint them. After some time to arrange for fees and supplies, Wangari's mother came to her. "You are going to school," she told her daughter.

Wangari grinned widely and hugged her mother. "Thank you!" she cried. "I will make you proud."

Wangari walked the long road to a one-room school-house with walls made of mud, a floor of dirt, and a roof of tin. In time, she learned to copy her letters and trace

numbers. Wangari's letters soon made words, and her words made sentences. She learned how numbers could be added and subtracted, multiplied and divided. Animals and plants, she discovered, were like human beings in many ways. They needed air, water, and nourishment, too.

When Wangari finished elementary school, she was eleven years old. Her mind was like a seed rooted in rich soil, ready to grow. Wangari wanted to continue her education, but to do so she would have to leave her village and move to the capital city of Nairobi. Wangari had never been farther than her valley's ridge. She was scared.

"Go," her mother said. She picked up a handful

of earth and placed it gently into her daughter's hand. "Where you go, we go."

Wangari was sad to leave, but she knew that what her mother said was true. Wherever Wangari went, so went her family, her village, and her Kikuyu ways. She kissed her family and said good-bye to the mugumo tree, remembering her promise to always protect it.

Going to School in Kenya

Before 1963, few Kenyan girls attended school. When Kenya won its independence from the United Kingdom (UK) that year, the new government began a campaign for free primary education and encouraged girls to go to school. Today, by law, boys and girls in Kenya must complete their early education and graduate from eighth grade.

Young students in Kenya attend public schools and private schools. A few wealthy Kenyan children go to boarding schools, where students live on the school's campus during the academic year and come home for their holiday breaks in April and August. No matter what kind of school they attend, all students have to get there on their own. Some are driven in cars or take buses while others ride their bikes or walk for miles.

A typical school day lasts from 8 a.m. until 4 p.m. with a break at noon for lunch. Many students bring their own lunch while some schools have a cafeteria. Students play sports such as soccer and cricket, a British game that is similar to baseball. Classes are held in both English and Swahili. Swahili, sometimes called

Classroom of young students from Maji Mazuri Centre and School, Nairobi, Kenya.

Kiswahili, is a language that's spoken in many countries in East Africa, including Kenya, Tanzania, and the Democratic Republic of the Congo.

The quality of education a student receives depends on where she lives, what type of school she attends, and the student-to-teacher ratio, which compares the number of students in a classroom to the number of teachers. Classes with smaller student-to-teacher ratios allow teachers to give more time and attention to each student, which can improve the students' quality of education. In some poor, rural areas, the ratio of teachers to students might be one teacher to every seventy-five or more students. In a wealthy suburb of Nairobi, the capital of Kenya, the ratio of teachers to students might be one to twenty-five or less. Generally, all students study the same subjects like math, reading, science, and history.

Some students in Kenya stop their schooling after eighth grade. This is more common among students from families who cannot afford school fees. Girls and boys may need to support their families by working in fields and factories instead of going to school. Others must take care of younger siblings while their parents work. Students who continue their education beyond eighth grade must take an exam to enter high school. Many of them go on to graduate from high school and attend colleges and universities.

CHAPTER THREE
BUDDING BRILLIANCE

Wangari's new life in the city amazed her. Skyscrapers towered above her head, not trees. People rushed through the streets like river water over stones. At school, she lived with other girls like her, all trying to weave their village customs with new city ones. At night when the girls slept, Wangari dreamed of home and the sweet figs of the mugumo tree. Her dreams reminded her to honor her Kikuyu tradition of respecting all living things.

Wangari was an excellent student, and science became her favorite subject. She especially loved studying living things. Air, she learned, was made from two **molecules** of oxygen bonded together. Bodies were made up of cells. Leaves changed color because of **photosynthesis**.

As graduation neared, Wangari told her friends she wanted to become a **biologist**.

"Not many native women become scientists," they told her.

"I will," she said.

Wangari would have to travel halfway around the world to the United States to study biology. She had never left Kenya and had little money. But with her teachers' help, she won a scholarship to a college in Kansas.

America was very different from Kenya. In college, many of Wangari's science professors were women. From them she learned that a woman could do anything she wanted to, even if it hadn't been done before. While Wangari discovered how molecules move under a microscope lens and how cells divide in **petri dishes**, she also found her strength as a woman scientist.

CHAPTER FOUR

THE SEEDS OF AN IDEA

After she graduated from college, Wangari traveled to Pennsylvania to continue her studies. Letters from home told Wangari about changes in Kenya. The people had elected a Kikuyu president, Jomo Kenyatta. Proud of her country and proud to be Kikuyu, Wangari decided to return home to Kenya to help her people.

America had changed Wangari. She had discovered a spirit of possibility and freedom that she wanted to share with Kenyan women. She accepted a teaching job at the University of Nairobi.

Not many women were professors then, and even fewer taught science. Wangari led the way for other women and girls. She worked for equal rights so that female scientists would be treated with the same respect as male scientists.

Wangari watched sadly as her government sold more and more land to big foreign companies that cut down forests for timber and to clear land for coffee plantations. Native trees such as cedar and acacia vanished. Without trees, birds had no place to nest. Monkeys lost their swings. Tired mothers walked miles for firewood.

When Wangari visited her village she saw that the Kikuyu custom of not chopping down the mugumo trees had been lost. No longer held in by tree roots, the soil streamed into the rivers. The water that had been used to grow maize, bananas, and sweet potatoes turned to mud and dried up. Many families went hungry.

Wangari could not bear to think of the land being destroyed. Now married and the mother of three children, she worried about what would happen to all the mothers and children who depended on the land.

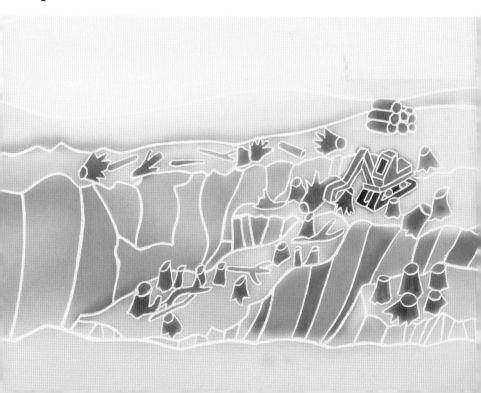

"We must do something," Wangari said.

Wangari had an idea as small as a seed but as tall as a tree that reaches for the sky.

"*Harambee!* Let's work together!" she said to her countrywomen—mothers like her. Wangari dug deep into the soil, a seedling by her side. "We must plant trees."

Many women listened. Many planted seedlings. Some men laughed and sneered. Planting trees was women's work, they said. Others complained that Wangari was too outspoken—with too many opinions and too much education for a woman.

Wangari refused to listen to those who criticized her.

Instead she told them, "the trees [you] are cutting down today were not planted by [you], but by those who came before. [You] must plant the trees that will benefit communities in the future. . . . [L]ike a seedling with sun, good soil, and abundant rain, the roots of our future will bury themselves in the ground and a **canopy** of hope will reach the sky."

Deforestation

Deforestation is the process of removing trees to create open land. It can happen naturally when trees fall in a landslide or burn down in a forest fire, but the most common cause of deforestation today is humans and their need to expand. People often cut down large wooded areas to build houses, factories, or shopping centers. Corporations also use trees for **timber** to make and sell paper or build houses.

Once the land has been cleared of trees, the local ecosystem is destroyed, which impacts other living **organisms**. Creatures such as birds, insects, and small animals lose their **habitats**, making it difficult for them to survive and increasing the chance of them becoming **extinct**. Without trees to break the wind or tree roots to hold on to the soil and water when it rains, erosion happens, leaving the land dry, dusty, and desert-like. In this way, deforestation can contribute to climate change.

Deforestation is a complicated problem. It mostly occurs in developing countries where there is a high level of poverty and low level of education. People need space to live, wood for building, and land for farming, all of which deforestation provides them.

For several decades, the needs of humans **out-weighed** the issues raised by deforestation. Now things are changing. People realize harming the environment hurts future generations. Environmentalists are working with developing countries to seek more **sustainable** ways to create housing, firewood, and jobs, without damaging the environment. Programs are practicing the powerful solution of *reforestation*. Reforestation is when people replant an area with trees so that the forest can regrow. It happens all over the world, in every country where forests have been cut down. Organizations like Greenpeace and the Sierra Club partner with young people and their communities to plant trees.

Smoke lingers after a fire in the Amazon rainforest along a riverbank in Ecuador, South America.

Wangari traveled to villages, towns, and cities with **saplings** and seeds, shovels and hoes. At each place she went, women planted rows of trees that looked like green belts across the land. Because of this, they started calling themselves the Green Belt Movement.

"We might not change the big world but we can change the landscape of the forest," she said.

One tree turned to ten, ten to one hundred, one hundred to one million, all the way up to thirty million planted trees. Kenya grew green again. Birds nested in new trees. Monkeys swung on branches. Rivers filled with clean water. Wild figs grew heavy in the mugumo's branches.

Mothers fed their children **maize**, bananas, and sweet potatoes until they could eat no more.

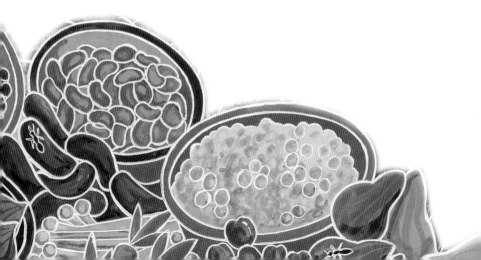

The Changing Roles of Women in Kenya

Kenya was under colonial rule by the United Kingdom for sixty-eight years, from 1895 until 1963. During that time, Kenyans were forced to obey the laws **imposed** upon them by the UK. People did not have the power to rule themselves, vote, or own land, and the Kenyan people suffered, especially women. Men, either fathers, brothers, or husbands, made decisions for the women and girls in their family, including who and when they married. Most women did not have professional careers, but farmed, took care of children, and stayed at home. Rarely did women work outside the house or did girls go to school. In 1963, Kenya became an independent nation and the Kenyan people had the power to create a free country for all—even for the women.

The roles of Kenyan women began to expand as they fought for access to higher education, healthcare, and affordable housing. In 1969, the first woman was elected to the newly formed Kenyan **Parliament**—evidence of the progress women were making. During the 1970s, Kenyan women joined other **activists** in the *women's rights movement*, a worldwide effort that involved people opposing laws and practices that discriminated against women based on their gender.

Women activists from Kenya, Uganda, Tanzania, Rwanda, and Burundi march in Nairobi, Kenya, to protest early marriage and all forms of violence and inequality against women, 2015.

Kenyan women continued to work together through the Green Belt Movement. The Green Belt Movement began in the late 1970s with a handful of women led by Wangari Maathai. Wangari and her team saw the devastating effects of deforestation and its impact on women who had to walk for miles for firewood and no longer had a stable food source. They decided that they would teach women how to plant trees. Each woman would be paid a small amount for the trees she planted and for caring for the trees. The group started out locally, helping women in rural areas, and turned into an international movement that influences young people and environmental organizations today worldwide.

Kenyan women continue to make strides toward better health care, against gender discrimination, and for equal opportunity in education and the workforce. Their progress over the last several decades is unmistakable. Today, Kenyan women have more opportunities to pursue the lives they want to lead.

CHAPTER FIVE

MOTHER OF TREES

As the Green Belt Movement moved farther across Kenya, powerful voices rose up against Wangari's movement. Foreign business people, greedy for more land for their coffee plantations and trees for timber, asked, "Who is this woman who can change so many lives with a sapling? Why should we give up our land and profits for trees?"

They made a plan to stop Wangari.

One day while she was out planting a tree, some wealthy businessmen paid corrupt police officers to arrest Wangari.

In her jail cell, Wangari prayed. And like a sturdy tree against a mighty wind, her faith kept her strong. Instead of giving up, she made friends with the other women prisoners. They told her their stories. She taught them about her seeds and saplings. Together, they helped one another.

Wangari knew many people in Kenya and other countries. They banded together to fight for her release. Before she was freed, Wangari promised to help fight for the rights of the other women prisoners, too.

Wangari realized that the people who had put her in jail didn't like the changes in the land or in the women. The people in charge of big companies wanted to keep the land for themselves, and the government was frightened of too many advances made by women. If she wanted to help save her country and countrywomen, Wangari would have to go out into the world to spread

her message. She would have to leave her home once more.

Wangari began to travel, telling her story to teachers, presidents, farmers, **ambassadors**, and schoolchildren all over the world. She dug in the dirt, planted seedlings, and spoke about women's rights. With everyone she met, she shared the seeds of change.

In time, Kenya changed. More people listened to Wangari's message, calling her the *Mama Miti*, "Mother of Trees." They wanted her to lead them into Kenya's new democracy. Wangari was elected to Kenya's parliament and became **minister** of the environment.

Still, she did not stop planting trees.

How to Plant a Tree

Planting trees is a fun and powerful way to fight climate change and learn more about how trees grow. Here are some basics you need to know if you want to plant a tree.

Planning Your Planting: Before you begin, you'll have to decide where to plant your tree. When picking a place, study how much natural sunlight, shade, and water is in that area. This will also help you decide what tree to get. You can buy a tree at your local garden store, order it online, or partner with an organization that gives away trees. The best time to plant a tree is usually during fall or spring so that the tree roots can settle into the soil before they are exposed to very hot weather in the summer or cold weather in the winter. Check with a local **arborist** for the best time of year to plant your tree.

Planting Your Tree: You will need a shovel, **mulch**, access to water, and your tree!

Before you dig, have an adult identify where underground **utilities** are located and make sure your digging and new tree will not damage them.

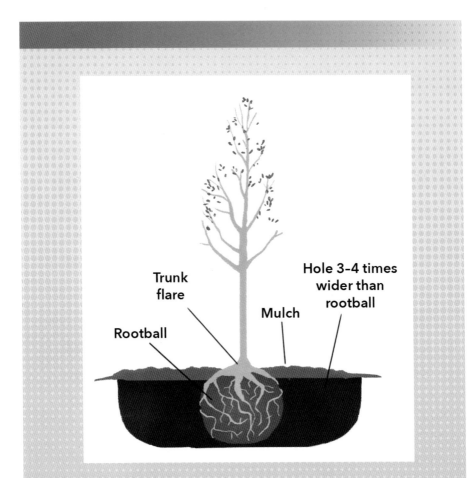

Trunk flare

Rootball

Mulch

Hole 3–4 times wider than rootball

With an adult's guidance, use the shovel to dig a hole that is three to four times wider than the container or burlap sack the tree came in. Set the dirt you dug up aside. Remove the tree from its container or burlap sack carefully so you don't rip the tree or yank out its roots. Place the tree root-end down in the middle of the hole. Use the soil you set aside to fill in the hole. Pack the soil around the sides of the tree to get rid of any air pockets. As you fill the hole with soil, make sure the tree is firmly planted and that the tree's trunk is pointing straight up. Give the tree a good drink of water, and then put a thick layer of mulch around the tree about four inches away from the trunk. Keep the mulch and soil moist but not overwatered.

Caring for Your Tree: Trees need to be watered during seasons when the weather is dry and hot. They also need to be protected from the cold during the winter. Ask a local arborist about the best way to care for your specific tree and to check on the health of your tree every two to three years.

You can connect with young people around the world who enjoy planting trees. Groups like Plant the Planet help students get involved with global justice and fight climate change. The group's goal is to plant one trillion trees worldwide! Get together with your friends and classmates to create your trees of change, like Wangari Maathai.

In 2004, at the age of sixty-four, Wangari won the most prestigious peace prize in the world, the Nobel Peace Prize. It had never before been awarded to an African woman or environmentalist.

The Green Belt Movement that Wangari founded in 1977 has spread globally, teaching people to take care of the environment by planting trees, recycling, and seeking alternative energy sources.

Standing in front of an audience of people from around the world, far from her village, Wangari remembered her girlhood lesson of the mugumo. She understood that persistence, patience, and commitment—to an idea as small as a seed but as tall as a tree that reaches the for the sky—must be planted in every child's heart.

"Young people, you are our hope and our future," she said.

And then, as she had done so many times before, Wangari planted a tree.

"Through the Green Belt Movement, we have helped young people get involved in environmental activities. We have tried to instill in them the idea that protecting the environment is not just a pleasure, but also a duty."

TIMELINE

1940 April 1: Wangari Muta born in Nyeri, Kenya

1948 Began attending the local primary school

1960 Selected to study in the US through a program sponsored by Senator John F. Kennedy. Traveled to the US to attend Mount St. Scholastica College (now Benedictine College) in Kansas

1964 Graduated from Mount St. Scholastica College with a degree in Biological Sciences

1966 Graduated from the University of Pittsburgh with a Master's degree in Biological Sciences

1966 Returned to Kenya

1967 Traveled to Germany to pursue doctoral studies at the University of Giessen and University of Munich

1968 Returned to Kenya to become a lecturer at the University College of Nairobi (now the University of Nairobi)

1969 Married Mwangi Mathai

1970 First of her three children born

1971 Graduated from the University College of

Nairobi with a doctorate in Veterinary Anatomy; she was the first Eastern African woman to receive a PhD

1977 Founded the Green Belt Movement

1979 Divorced Mwangi Mathai; when he demanded she drop his last name, she chose to add a second "a" instead

1982 Planned to run for Parliament, but was disqualified based on a technicality; began to focus on Green Belt action full-time

1986-1989 The Green Belt Movement spreads throughout Africa

1992 Arrested for pro-democracy activism; the charges are dropped later that year

1997 Unsuccessfully ran for Parliament and the presidency of Kenya

2002 Elected to Parliament

2003 Appointed Assistant Minister in the Ministry for Environment and Natural Resources; published her book *The Green Belt Movement: Sharing the Approach and the Experience*

2004 Received the Nobel Peace Prize

2008 Published her memoir, *Unbowed*

2009 Named a UN Messenger of Peace by the United Nations Secretary-General

2010 Founded the Wangari Maathai Institute for Peace and Environmental Studies

2011 September 25: Died, in Nairobi, Kenya, at age 71

GLOSSARY

activist (AK-tih-vist) *noun* a person who publicly supports or takes action to bring change to a society and government

ambassador (am-BA-sah-door) *noun* a high-ranking government official who represents their country within the territory of a different country

aquatic (uh-KWAH-tik) *adjective* living in water

arborist (AR-bor-ist) *noun* a person who specializes in caring for trees

asthma (AZ-muh) *noun* a physical condition that makes it difficult to breathe

beckon (BEH-kun) *verb* to gesture someone over to you using your hand or head

biodiversity (BI-oh-di-VER-sih-tee) *noun* a wide variety of plants and animals living in one environment

biologist (bi-OL-oh-jist) *noun* a person who studies biology, the science of living things

canopy (KAN-oh-pee) *noun* a cover made of cloth or another thin material used as a roof

carbon dioxide (KAR-bun dy-OKS-eyed) *noun* a gas made of carbon and oxygen that animals breathe out and plants take in

coexist (KO-ek-zist) *verb* to exist in the same place as another living thing

drastically (DRAH-stik-lee) *adverb* severely

erosion (err-OH-shun) *noun* the gradual process of the earth's surface being worn away by natural forces, such as wind and rain

extinct (EKS-tinkt) *adjective* no longer surviving or existing

habitat (HAB-eh-tat) *noun* the type of place where a plant or animal is naturally found

impose (im-POZE) *verb* force

interdependent (IN-ter-DEE-pen-dant) *adjective* relying on one another for survival

maize (MAZE) *noun* corn

millet (MILL-it) *noun* certain grasses that are grown for their seeds, often used for food

minister (MIN-is-tur) *noun* an official who oversees a specific topic or area of government

molecule (MAH-leh-kewl) *noun* a particle composed of two or more atoms that together create the smallest possible amount of a substance

mulch (MULCH) *noun* a combination of leaves, compost, wood pieces, and other materials that is spread on the ground to help keep the soil beneath it moist and prevent weeds from growing

nourishment (NOR-ish-mint) *noun* food and other substances needed for a healthy life and growth

nutrient (NEW-tree-ent) *noun* a substance that living things need to grow and be healthy

organic (or-GAN-ik) *adjective* having to do with living things

organisms (or-GAN-iz-ims) *noun* living things

outweigh (OWT-way) *verb* to be more important or greater than something else

parliament (PAR-lah-mint) *noun* the national legislature in some countries, much like the US Congress

petri dish (PEE-tree DISH) *noun* a small, shallow bowl made of clear plastic or glass used in a science lab to contain and study small amounts of something

photosynthesis (fo-toh-SIN-theh-sis) *noun* the process by which plants use sunlight to make food

sapling (SAP-pling) *noun* a young tree

sustainable (sus-TAIN-uh-bull) *adjective* involving ways that do not harm the natural environment

timber (TIM-burr) *noun* wood

ultraviolet light (ULL-trah-VI-lit LIGHT) *noun* rays of

light that cannot be seen by humans because
they exist beyond the violet end of the visible
light spectrum

utilities (yoo-TIL-lit-tees) *noun* electricity, water, gas, or
sewage services

TEXT SOURCES

Fowler, Susanne. "Arrest of Kenya Leader Maathai Draws Fire." *Chicago Tribune.* January 26, 1992. https://www.chicagotribune.com/news/ct-xpm-1992-01-26-9201080534-story.html.

Frängsmyr, Tore, ed. "Wangari Maathai Biographical." NobelPrize.org. https://www.nobelprize.org/prizes/peace/2004/maathai/biographical/.

The Green Belt Movement. "Biography." The Green Belt Movement. https://www.greenbeltmovement.org/wangari-maathai/biography.

Maathai, Wangari. *The Green Belt Movement: Sharing the Approach and the Experience.* New York: Lantern Books, 2006.

———. *Unbowed: A Memoir.* London: Arrow Books, 2009.

QUOTATION SOURCES

p. 15: "Why . . . school?" *Unbowed: A Memoir* by Wangari Maathai, p. 40.

p. 30: "The trees . . . the sky." Ibid., p. 289.

p. 48: "persistence, patience, and commitment" *The Green Belt Movement: Sharing the Approach and the Experience* by Wangari Maathai, p. 12.

p. 48: "Young people . . . our future."
Adapted from the transcript of Wangari Maathai's Nobel Lecture: http://nobelprize.org/nobel_prizes/peace/laureates/2004/maathai-lecture-text.html.

SIDEBAR SOURCES

TREES AND THE FOREST ECOSYSTEM

"Fun Facts for Kids on Animals, Earth, History and More!" DK Find Out! Accessed June 19, 2019. https://www.dkfindout.com/us/animals-and-nature/plants/trees/.

Ingoglia, Gina. *The Tree Book: For Kids and Their Grown-ups*. Brooklyn, NY: Brooklyn Botanic Garden, 2016.

PBS. "Learning about Trees." Adventures in Learning with Jennifer Cooper. Accessed October 21, 2013. https://www.pbs.org/video/ adventures-learning-learn-about-trees/.

THE EDUCATION SYSTEM IN KENYA

"Education in Kenya." World Education News & Reviews. December 17, 2018. Accessed June 19, 2019. https://wenr.wes.org/2015/06/education-kenya.

National Geographic Society. "Kenya." National Geographic Kids. June 14, 2019. Accessed June 19, 2019. https://kids.nationalgeographic.com/explore/countries/kenya/.

DEFORESTATION

"Deforestation and Forest Degradation." WWF. Accessed June 19, 2019. https://www.worldwildlife.org/threats/deforestation-and-forest-degradation.

Nunez, Christina. "Deforestation, Explained." National Geographic. February 7, 2019. "Deforestation and Its Effect on the Planet." https://www.nationalgeographic.com/environment/global-warming/deforestation/.

THE CHANGING ROLES OF WOMEN IN KENYA

"Kenya." UN Women. Accessed June 19, 2019. http://africa.unwomen.org/en/where-we-are/eastern-and-southern-africa/kenya.

Maathai, Wangari. *The Green Belt Movement: Sharing the Approach and the Experience*. New York, NY: Lantern Books, 2006.

———. *Unbowed: A Memoir*. London, UK: Arrow Books, 2009.

Swift, Jaimee A. "African Women and Social Movements in Africa." Black Perspectives. July 18, 2017. https://www.aaihs.org/african-women-and-social-movements-in-africa/.

HOW TO PLANT A TREE

"How to Plant Balled and Burlapped Trees." Arbor Day Foundation. Accessed June 19, 2019. https://www.arborday.org/trees/planting/balled-burlapped.cfm.

"How to Plant Containerized Trees." Arbor Day Foundation. Accessed June 19, 2019. https://www.arborday.org/trees/planting/containerized.cfm.

Plant for the Planet. Accessed June 19, 2019. https://www.plant-for-the-planet.org/en/home.

RECOMMENDED FURTHER READING AND RESOURCES

Fiction books are marked with an asterisk.

WOMEN IN SCIENCE

*Choldenko, Gennifer. *Chasing Secrets*. New York: Penguin, 2016.

Ignotofsky, Rachel. *Women in Science: 50 Fearless Pioneers Who Changed the World*. New York: Penguin Random House, 2016.

Shetterly, Margot Lee. *Hidden Figures*. Young Readers' Edition. New York: HarperCollins Children's Books, 2016.

Silvey, Anita. *Untamed: The Wild of Jane Goodall*. Boone, IA: National Geographic Children's Books, 2015.

ACTIVISM

Clinton, Chelsea. *It's Your World: Get Informed, Get Inspired & Get Going!* New York: Philomel/Penguin, 2017.

*Hiaasen, Carl. *Hoot*. New York: Penguin, 2005.

Hopkins, Joseph H. *The Tree Lady: The True Story of How One Tree-Loving Woman Changed a City Forever*. New York: Simon & Schuster, 2013.

Hopkinson, Deborah. *What is the Women's Rights*

Movement? What Was? series. New York: Penguin, 2018.

Thompson, Laurie Ann. *Be a Changemaker: How to Start Something That Matters.* New York: Simon & Schuster, 2014.

NOBEL PEACE PRIZE WINNERS

Abouraya, Karen Leggett. *Malala Yousafzai: Warrior with Words.* New York: Lee & Low Books, 2019.

Gigliotti, Jim. *Who Was Mother Teresa?* Who Was? series. New York: Penguin, 2015.

Stone, Tanya Lee. *The House That Jane Built: A Story About Jane Addams.* New York: Henry Holt/Macmillan, 2015.

Yoo, Paula. *The Story of Banker of the People Muhammad Yunus.* New York: Lee & Low Books, 2019.

The Green Belt Movement: https://www.greenbeltmovement.org.

Greenpeace: https://www.greenpeace.org/usa/.

Plant for the Planet: https://www.plant-for-the-planet.org/en/home.

The Sierra Club: https://www.sierraclub.org/home.

United States Environmental Protection Agency (EPA): https://www.epa.gov.

ABOUT THE AUTHOR AND ILLUSTRATOR

JEN CULLERTON JOHNSON is a writer, an educator, and an environmentalist with master's degrees in nonfiction writing and curriculum development. She has taught in countries all around the world and now teaches at an inner-city elementary school in Chicago, where she also conducts writing workshops. She was inspired by Wangari Maathai's dedication to women and the environment. Johnson can be found online at jencullertonjohnson.com.

SONIA LYNN SADLER was an illustrator and a fine artist. Growing up, she traveled to many countries and lived in five different states. Eventually landing in Maryland and later New Jersey, Sadler focused on depicting the cultures, lives, and stories of peoples of African descent. Her book *Seeds of Change* earned her a Coretta Scott King/ John Steptoe Award for New Talent. Her unique style employed a variety of techniques and mediums—from watercolor to scratchboard—and drew inspiration from quilts. She passed away in September 2013. The Sonia Lynn Sadler Award for Illustration is an annual prize that honors diversity in illustrated children's books.